D0996672

Francis Frith's

AROUND CAMBRIDGE

◆

PHOTOGRAPHIC MEMORIES

Francis Frith's

AROUND CAMBRIDGE

◆

Clive Tully

First published in the United Kingdom in 1999 by The Francis Frith Collection

Hardback Edition 1999
ISBN 1-85937-092-6

Paperback Edition 2001
ISBN 1-85937-422-0

Reprinted in Hardback 2005

Reprinted in Paperback 2005

Text and Design copyright The Francis Frith Collection®
Photographs copyright The Francis Frith Collection®
except where indicated.

The Frith® photographs and the Frith® logo are reproduced under licence
from Heritage Photographic Resources Ltd, the owners of the Frith® archive
and trademarks. 'The Francis Frith Collection', 'Francis Frith' and 'Frith' are
registered trademarks of Heritage Photographic Resources Ltd.

All rights reserved. No photograph in this publication may be sold to a
third party other than in the original form of this publication, or framed
for sale to a third party. No parts of this publication may be reproduced,
stored in a retrieval system, or transmitted, in any form, or by any means,
electronic, mechanical, photocopying, recording or otherwise, without the
prior permission of the publishers and copyright holder.

British Library Cataloguing in Publication Data

Cambridge - Photographic Memories
Clive Tully
ISBN 1-85937-092-6

The Francis Frith Collection
Frith's Barn, Teffont,
Salisbury, Wiltshire SP3 5QP
Tel: +44 (0) 1722 716 376
Email: info@francisfrith.co.uk
www.francisfrith.co.uk

Printed and bound in Great Britain

Front Cover: CAMBRIDGE, Petty Cury 1909 61469t

*The colour-tinting is for illustrative purposes only, and is not intended
to be historically accurate*

Aerial photographs reproduced under licence from
Simmons Aerofilms Limited.
Historical Ordnance Survey maps reproduced under licence from
Homecheck.co.uk

Every attempt has been made to contact copyright holders of illustrative
material. We will be happy to give full acknowledgement in future editions
for any items not credited. Any information should be directed to
The Francis Frith Collection.

AS WITH ANY HISTORICAL DATABASE THE FRITH ARCHIVE IS
CONSTANTLY BEING CORRECTED AND IMPROVED AND THE
PUBLISHERS WOULD WELCOME INFORMATION ON OMISSIONS
OR INACCURACIES

CONTENTS

FRANCIS FRITH: *Victorian Pioneer*

FRANCIS FRITH, Victorian founder of the world-famous photographic archive, was a complex and multitudinous man. A devout Quaker and a highly successful Victorian businessman, he was both philosophical by nature and pioneering in outlook.

By 1855 Francis Frith had already established a wholesale grocery business in Liverpool, and sold it for the astonishing sum of £200,000, which is the equivalent today of over £15,000,000. Now a very rich man, he was able to indulge his passion for travel. As a child he had pored over travel books written by early explorers, and his fancy and imagination had been stirred by family holidays to the sublime mountain regions of Wales and Scotland. 'What lands of spirit-stirring and enriching scenes and places!' he had written. He was to return to these scenes of grandeur in later years to 'recapture the thousands of vivid and tender memories', but with a different purpose. Now in his thirties, and captivated by the new science of photography, Frith set out on a series of pioneering journeys to the Nile regions that occupied him from 1856 until 1860.

INTRIGUE AND ADVENTURE

He took with him on his travels a specially-designed wicker carriage that acted as both dark-room and sleeping chamber. These far-flung journeys were packed with intrigue and adventure. In his life story, written when he was sixty-three, Frith tells of being held captive by bandits, and of fighting 'an awful midnight battle to the very point of surrender with a deadly pack of hungry, wild dogs'. Sporting flowing Arab costume, Frith arrived at Akaba by camel sixty years before Lawrence, where he encountered 'desert princes and rival sheikhs, blazing with jewel-hilted swords'.

During these extraordinary adventures he was assiduously exploring the desert regions bordering the Nile and patiently recording the antiquities and peoples with his camera. He was the first photographer to venture beyond the sixth cataract. Africa was still the mysterious 'Dark Continent', and Stanley and Livingstone's historic meeting was a decade into the future. The conditions for picture taking confound belief. He laboured for hours in his wicker dark-room in the sweltering heat of the desert, while the volatile chemicals fizzed dangerously in their trays. Often he was forced to work in remote tombs and caves where conditions were cooler. Back in London he

exhibited his photographs and was 'rapturously cheered' by members of the Royal Society. His reputation as a photographer was made overnight. An eminent modern historian has likened their impact on the population of the time to that on our own generation of the first photographs taken on the surface of the moon.

VENTURE OF A LIFE-TIME

Characteristically, Frith quickly spotted the opportunity to create a new business as a specialist publisher of photographs. He lived in an era of immense and sometimes violent change. For the poor in the early part of Victoria's reign work was a drudge and the hours long, and people had precious little free time to enjoy themselves. Most had no transport other than a cart or

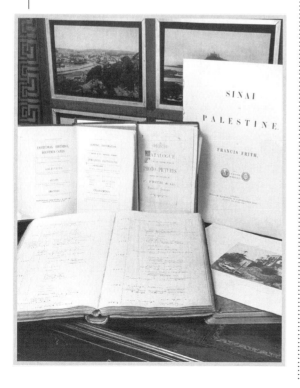

gig at their disposal, and had not travelled far beyond the boundaries of their own town or village. However, by the 1870s, the railways had threaded their way across the country, and Bank Holidays and half-day Saturdays had been made obligatory by Act of Parliament. All of a sudden the ordinary working man and his family were able to enjoy days out and see a little more of the world.

With characteristic business acumen, Francis Frith foresaw that these new tourists would enjoy having souvenirs to commemorate their days out. In 1860 he married Mary Ann Rosling and set out with the intention of photographing every city, town and village in Britain. For the next thirty years he travelled the country by train and by pony and trap, producing fine photographs of seaside resorts and beauty spots that were keenly bought by millions of Victorians. These prints were painstakingly pasted into family albums and pored over during the dark nights of winter, rekindling precious memories of summer excursions.

THE RISE OF FRITH & CO

Frith's studio was soon supplying retail shops all over the country. To meet the demand he gathered about him a small team of photographers, and published the work of independent artist-photographers of the calibre of Roger Fenton and Francis Bedford. In order to gain some understanding of the scale of Frith's business one only has to look at the catalogue issued by Frith & Co in 1886: it runs to some 670 pages, listing not only many thousands

of views of the British Isles but also many photographs of most European countries, and China, Japan, the USA and Canada – note the sample page shown above from the hand-written *Frith & Co* ledgers detailing pictures taken. By 1890 Frith had created the greatest specialist photographic publishing company in the world, with over 2,000 outlets – more than the combined number that Boots and WH Smith have today! The picture on the right shows the *Frith & Co* display board at Ingleton in the Yorkshire Dales (left of window). Beautifully constructed with a mahogany frame and gilt inserts, it could display up to a dozen local scenes.

POSTCARD BONANZA

The ever-popular holiday postcard we know today took many years to develop. In 1870 the Post Office issued the first plain cards, with a pre-printed stamp on one face. In 1894 they allowed other publishers' cards to be sent through the mail with an attached adhesive halfpenny stamp. Demand grew rapidly, and in 1895 a new size of postcard was permitted called the court card, but there was little room for illustration. In

1899, a year after Frith's death, a new card measuring 5.5 x 3.5 inches became the standard format, but it was not until 1902 that the divided back came into being, with address and message on one face and a full-size illustration on the other. *Frith & Co* were in the vanguard of postcard development, and Frith's sons Eustace and Cyril continued their father's monumental task, expanding the number of views offered to the public and recording more and more places in Britain, as the coasts and countryside were opened up to mass travel.

Francis Frith died in 1898 at his villa in Cannes, his great project still growing. The archive he created continued in business for another seventy years. By 1970 it contained over a third of a million pictures of 7,000 cities, towns and villages. The massive photographic record Frith has left to us stands as a living monument to a special and very remarkable man.

Frith's Archive: *A Unique Legacy*

FRANCIS FRITH'S legacy to us today is of immense significance and value, for the magnificent archive of evocative photographs he created provides a unique record of change in 7,000 cities, towns and villages throughout Britain over a century and more. Frith and his fellow studio photographers revisited locations many times down the years to update their views, compiling for us an enthralling and colourful pageant of British life and character.

We tend to think of Frith's sepia views of Britain as nostalgic, for most of us use them to conjure up memories of places in our own lives with which we have family associations. It often makes us forget that to Francis Frith they were records of daily life as it was actually being lived in the cities, towns and villages of his day. The Victorian age was one of great and often bewildering change for ordinary people, and though the pictures evoke an impression of slower times, life was as busy and hectic as it is today.

We are fortunate that Frith was a photographer of the people, dedicated to recording the minutiae of everyday life. For it is this sheer wealth of visual data, the painstaking chronicle of changes in dress, transport, street layouts, buildings, housing, engineering and landscape that captivates us so much today. His remarkable images offer us a powerful link with the past and with the lives of our ancestors.

TODAY'S TECHNOLOGY

Computers have now made it possible for Frith's many thousands of images to be accessed almost instantly. In the Frith archive today, each photograph is carefully 'digitised' then stored on a CD Rom. Frith archivists can locate a single photograph amongst thousands within seconds. Views can be catalogued and sorted under a variety of categories of place and content to the immediate benefit of researchers. Inexpensive reference prints can be created for them at the touch of a mouse button, and a wide range of books and other printed materials assembled and published for a wider, more general readership - in the next twelve months over a hundred Frith local history titles will be published!

See Frith at www. francisfrith.co.uk

The day-to-day workings of the archive are very different from how they were in Francis Frith's time: imagine the herculean task of sorting through eleven tons of glass negatives as Frith had to do to locate a particular sequence of pictures! Yet the archive still prides itself on maintaining the same high standards of excellence laid down by Francis Frith, including the painstaking cataloguing and indexing of every view.

It is curious to reflect on how the internet now allows researchers in America and elsewhere greater instant access to the archive than Frith himself ever enjoyed. Many thousands of individual views can be called up on screen within seconds on one of the Frith internet sites, enabling people living continents away to revisit the streets of their ancestral home town, or view places in Britain where they have enjoyed holidays. Many overseas researchers welcome the chance to view special theme selections, such as transport, sports, costume and ancient monuments.

We are certain that Francis Frith would have heartily approved of these modern developments, for he himself was always working at the very limits of Victorian photographic technology.

THE VALUE OF THE ARCHIVE TODAY

Because of the benefits brought by the computer, Frith's images are increasingly studied by social historians, by researchers into genealogy and ancestory, by architects, town planners, and by teachers and schoolchildren involved in local history projects. In addition, the archive offers every one of us a unique opportunity to examine the places where we and our families have lived and worked down the years. Immensely successful in Frith's own era, the archive is now, a century and more on, entering a new phase of popularity.

THE PAST IN TUNE WITH THE FUTURE

Historians consider the Francis Frith Collection to be of prime national importance. It is the only archive of its kind remaining in private ownership and has been valued at a million pounds. However, this figure is now rapidly increasing as digital technology enables more and more people around the world to enjoy its benefits.

Francis Frith's archive is now housed in an historic timber barn in the beautiful village of Teffont in Wiltshire. Its founder would not recognize the archive office as it is today. In place of the many thousands of dusty boxes containing glass plate negatives and an all-pervading odour of photographic chemicals, there are now ranks of computer screens. He would be amazed to watch his images travelling round the world at unimaginable speeds through network and internet lines.

The archive's future is both bright and exciting. Francis Frith, with his unshakeable belief in making photographs available to the greatest number of people, would undoubtedly approve of what is being done today with his lifetime's work. His photographs, depicting our shared past, are now bringing pleasure and enlightenment to millions around the world a century and

CAMBRIDGE – *An Introduction*

CAMBRIDGE NATURALLY SPRINGS to mind as a great seat of learning; but the city's - or town's as it was until the 1950s - history goes back much further than the colleges, and was founded on principles far more commercial than academic. Although the site of encampments of various military interests from the Romans onwards, its major importance was due to its position at the head of navigation on the River Cam, or Granta, as it was known originally, making it an ideal trading centre. When the college buildings did start to appear, it was this position on the Fenland waterways which allowed the extravagant use of building materials not normally found in the region.

William the Conqueror built a castle here in 1068 as a forward position for his campaign against Hereward the Wake, leader of a guerilla campaign against the Normans after the invasion. Nevertheless, Hereward fought on for another three years from his base in the Isle of Ely before finally being overcome. Religious orders began to spring up, and it was probably as a result of these that the first colleges came about; in fact, they owed their existence to the older institutions in Oxford.

We do know that in 1209 some scholars, having to leave Oxford in rather a hurry after some trouble with the townsfolk, came to Cambridge. Some of their number had been accused of murder and were hanged in Oxford by the townspeople, with the approval of King John.

While many of them returned to Oxford when the fuss had died down five years later, enough of them remained for them to form a scholastic community. By the mid-13th century, this gathering of students and teachers was recognised as a University, despite the fact that they had no buildings of their own. In 1284, the first college was built next to a church called St Peter's, and was duly named Peterhouse by its founder, Hugh de Balsam, the Bishop of Ely.

The next two hundred years saw the addition of other colleges, and as they expanded, so did their powers. The University acquired the right to inspect weights and measures, in order that traders could not take advantage of the students. They even had their own courts, which could try offenders against members of the University. Not surprisingly, these powers, although rarely abused, led to unrest between town and gown (the townsfolk and the University). When Henry VI started planning the building of King's College in 1441, he had a large number of buildings removed, including a church - a move which would hardly have gone down very well at the time. Similarly, the Backs, the peaceful gardens backing onto the river behind the colleges, were once common land on which the townsfolk grazed their sheep. The money which wealthy

After Peterhouse was founded, there followed a succession of colleges, set up by a variety of people with different motives. King's Hall (which later became part of Trinity College) was founded by Edward III for the choristers of the Chapel Royal. Pembroke, set up by Marie de Valence, the French Countess of Pembroke, was the first college in Cambridge to have its own chapel (the present one was built in 1663 by Christopher Wren). In the 15th century came the Royal College

benefactors endowed on the various colleges was used tastefully, enhancing the town with a magnificent architectural heritage.

For centuries, Oxford and Cambridge were England's only universities. In medieval times, students would enter the university at the age of fourteen, and stay until they were twenty-one, or sometimes older. The minimum seven-year course culminated in an MA or BA degree. Before there were any college buildings, tutors lectured in borrowed halls and churches, while their students took what lodgings they could in the town. They would frequent the taverns, drinking, causing disturbances, and often enraging the townsfolk.

of the Blessed Virgin Mary and St Nicholas of Canterbury, subsequently known as King's, founded by Henry VI. He had already set up Eton College in Windsor, and the new college would have its scholars drawn from there. As with Eton, his first concern was the establishment of a chapel, the design of which would be modelled more on the lines of a cathedral choir rather than the buildings typical of college chapels so far - this was the reason why the King's master mason, Reginald of Ely, was appointed as architect. Building started in 1446, but came to a premature stop with the Wars of the Roses; after Henry's death, it fell to Edward IV and Henry VII to continue the building, with Henry VIII overseeing the finishing touches in 1513. While monastic properties fell to Henry VIII's Reformation, the colleges of Cambridge remained secure. In fact, the king even used the proceeds of dissolved religious establishments to set up his own college, when he merged Michaelhouse and King's Hall into Trinity College.

Many students who have passed through the University throughout the ages have helped shape events in history - Oliver Cromwell, Samuel Pepys, Isaac Newton, Charles Darwin, Milton, Tennyson, Wordsworth and Byron. Cromwell, a student at Sidney Sussex College, later became MP for Cambridge, and during the Civil War he made the town his headquarters for the Eastern Association.

Of the many Cambridge men who sailed to America in the 17th century, one was John Harvard, a graduate of Emmanuel College. He died in 1638 in Massachusetts, leaving half his estate to the school which had just been set up in Newetowne - subsequently renamed Cambridge in recognition of the fact that around seventy of the colony's founders had been educated there. The following year, the college was named Harvard in his honour.

In the mid-19th century, Cambridge's population numbered around thirty thousand people, with the parishes of Trumpington, Cherry Hinton and Chesterton still separate from the town. Living conditions were far from perfect, with open drains in the streets, and the River Cam nothing more than a sewer, while many townsfolk lived in slum accommodation. But the arrival of the railway in the 1840s brought not just more people, but industry and housing, swallowing up some of those outlying villages.

Today, Cambridge is a centre of technology, with its Science Park and the so-called 'Silicon Fen', a concentration of companies and organisations specialising in computer technology, many of them benefiting from the research carried on in the University. But despite all this, the centre of Cambridge itself retains its spirit of a market town. Add to that its grand college buildings, narrow streets and alleyways, together with the peaceful open greens and the river, and you have a place with a dignified charm which is unique among British towns and cities.

St John's College 1908 60849

The early Tudor gateway of St John's College is richly decorated with the arms of its founder, Lady Margaret Beaufort. The gatehouse leads to the First Court, and beyond come the Second and Third Courts, each younger than the previous one.

Queens' College 1890 26572

Queens' College was founded in 1448. It was one of the first colleges to be built in red brick at the time when the rather expensive fashion of imported stone began to decline. The second court contains the President's Lodge, one of the few half-timbered Tudor college buildings.

CLARE COLLEGE 1890 26568
Here we see Clare College from
Clare Bridge, which dates from
1640: it is the oldest surviving
bridge in Cambridge. Generations
of visitors have been asked the
same question: 'How many balls
are there on the balustrades?'

TRINITY COLLEGE 1914 66872a
Trinity College's Great Court, built between 1593 and 1615, is the largest university quadrangle in Europe.
The fountain in the centre was built at the beginning of the 17th century by Italian craftsmen.

MAGDALENE COLLEGE 1909 61494
Magdalene College was founded by Henry VI as lodgings for student Benedictine monks, and was sited far
enough from the town centre to avoid its inmates falling prey to its temptations. It became a college in 1542.
Samuel Pepys studied here between 1650 and 1653, and on his death in 1703 his library came here, including
the original manuscript volumes of his famous diaries. The best known Master of Magdalene College is A C
Benson, who wrote 'Land of Hope and Glory'.

EMMANUEL COLLEGE 1914 66858
Emmanuel College was originally the site of a Dominican friary. After the dissolution came a short period of disuse before Sir Walter Mildmay restored parts of the friary for use as a college. The chapel is another example of Wren's work; it shows Italian influences. One student at Emmanuel, John Harvard, emigrated to America, where the famous university in Massachusetts was named after him.

TRINITY COLLEGE LIBRARY 1890 26490
Trinity College's magnificent library was designed by Christopher Wren 1676-90, with wood carvings by Grinling Gibbons. The statue at the end is of Lord Byron. The library houses many famous manuscripts, including ones by Milton, Macaulay, Thackeray and Tennyson.

JESUS COLLEGE 1890 26530

Jesus College grew from a 12th-century convent. James I visited the college, and was so impressed by its tranquil surroundings that he said, given the choice, that he would 'pray at King's, dine at Trinity, and study and sleep at Jesus'.

PEMBROKE COLLEGE 1890 26547

This view looks north along Trumpington Street, with Pembroke College on the right, and Peterhouse on the left. Pembroke College was founded in 1347, and is significant in that it was here that Christopher Wren first translated a design from the drawing board into stone. It was commissioned by Wren's uncle, the Bishop of Ely, who after spending eighteen years in prison, decided that a building would be a fitting way to celebrate his release!

PEMBROKE COLLEGE 1955

Sixty-five years on from photograph No 26547, and not very much has changed, save for the more abundant foliage, and Trumpington Street now echoing to the sound of cars! Even now, you cannot help noticing the particularly deep gutters lining the road. They were installed in the 17th century, in an attempt to improve the city's water supply.

◆

ST CATHARINE'S COLLEGE 1890

St Catharine's College's open court faces Trumpington Street. The chapel houses a memorial to one of its more famous alumni, John Addenbrooke, whose bequest founded the county hospital.

PEMBROKE COLLEGE 1955 C14060

ST CATHARINE'S COLLEGE 1890 26601

PETERHOUSE 1890 26585

Peterhouse is distinguished as the first college in Cambridge, although the original 13th-century buildings have been altered considerably. Matthew Wren (Christopher's uncle) was master here from 1625-34, and he was responsible for the chapel, which combines Perpendicular and classical styles.

GIRTON COLLEGE 1908 60812

Cambridge's first women's college started out in Hitchin in 1869, and was moved to Girton three years later - sufficiently far removed from Cambridge and the temptations of its male students. But while these red-brick buildings offered women higher education, it was only fifty years later that women became entitled to receive degrees.

ENTRANCE TO SELWYN COLLEGE 1923 73520
Selwyn College was designed in the Tudor Gothic style by Sir Arthur Blomfield. It was established as a theological college in 1882 as a memorial to George Augustus Selwyn, who was the first Bishop of New Zealand, and later Bishop of Lichfield.

ST CATHARINE'S COLLEGE DINING HALL 1914 66867
St Catharine's was founded by Robert Woodlarke in 1473, then the third provost of King's. He came from a wealthy family, and spent much of his fortune developing St Catharine's (named after the patron saint of learning). None of the original buildings survive, however, and most of the structure, including the magnificent dining hall, is 17th-century or later.

Christ's College

TRINITY HALL 1909 61476

Not part of Trinity College, but a college in its own right, Trinity Hall was founded in 1350 by William Bateman, Bishop of Norwich. Initially set up to train priests, for centuries it was the place of excellence for people studying law.

NEWNHAM COLLEGE 1890 26542

Newnham College was Cambridge's second college for women, and was built a lot closer to the centre than the first one at Girton. It originally started as just five women students assembling in a house in Cambridge to be tutored by Mrs Jemima Clough; as the establishment grew, it moved into a building in the suburb of Newnham, taking that name for the college. When the Liberal politician W E Gladstone visited the college three years previously, the occasion was celebrated with the planting of a tree. Shortly afterwards it was uprooted by Tory undergraduates!

KING'S COLLEGE CHAPEL AND GATEWAY 1933 85551
Pictured here from King's Parade, the gatehouse which leads into the Front Court of King's College was built in 1828 by William Wilkins. Beyond is the Chapel, unsurpassed in its magnificence, with the largest and most complete set of ancient windows in the world.

SEDGEWICK AVENUE, UNIVERSITY DEPARTMENTS c1965 C14132
The cars look quaint and characterful, but these days the typical post-war architecture seems tired in style and not a lot more than simply functional.

Petty Cury

Petty Cury 1909

MARKET PLACE 1938 88526
The Market Square has a tradition going back to the early Middle Ages, although the present Square replaces houses destroyed by a fire in 1849. With stalls creaking under the weight of locally grown produce, there is no hint of the rationing to come after the outbreak of war the following year.

THE GUILDHALL 1890 26616
Ornate decoration can be seen inside the grand main hall of Cambridge's Guildhall. It was not just the scene of civic functions, but of musical events as well.

THE GUILDHALL 1938

The present Guildhall building, with its clean neo-Georgian styling, replaced the earlier one on the south side of the market square in 1936-7.

◆

ADDENBROOKE'S HOSPITAL 1938

When Dr John Addenbrooke died in 1719, he left over £4,500 to build a new hospital. Here we see Addenbrooke's from the roof of the Fitzwilliam Museum in Trumpington Street. Today's hospital is a vast complex on the southern outskirts of Cambridge, renowned for its special skills in dealing with head injuries.

THE GUILDHALL 1938 88521

ADDENBROOKE'S HOSPITAL 1938 88528

Fitzwilliam Museum

HOBBS'S PAVILION 1931 84523

Born in Cambridge in 1882, Sir John Berry 'Jack' Hobbs was undoubtedly the world's greatest cricket batsman of his time. Between 1905 and 1934 he played in 61 test matches and scored a record 61,237 runs. Perhaps his greatest innings at the Oval was against Australia in 1926, when he made a century to help bring back the Ashes to England. Hobbs's Pavilion on Parker's Piece, (note the batsman wind vane), honours Cambridge's sporting son. These days, Hobbs's Pavilion is a restaurant.

FENNER'S CRICKET GROUND 1921 70615a

Fenner's cricket ground is the University cricket ground. Nearby Parker's Piece is where the local non-university clubs play, and where Jack Hobbs developed his skills before gaining fame in national and international cricket.

MARKET PLACE 1890 26617
Perhaps not on a par with the great Suffolk wool churches, Great St Mary's, overlooking the Market Place, is none the less an impressive piece of Perpendicular architecture. Many great clerics have preached here, including Latimer, Ridley and Cranmer.

THE BANK AND POST OFFICE 1931 84537
Looking down towards St Andrew's Street, with First Court, the oldest part of Christ's College, in the distance. The Capital and Counties bank (now Lloyd's) and Post Office are in the foreground.

MARKET PLACE 1938 88527

Here we see the Market Place from the Guildhall. The number of parked cars is perhaps an indication of the traffic problems to come in later years.

HILLS ROAD 1931 84529

The war memorial is situated on the junction of Station Road with Hills Road. Dedicated by the Duke of York (or rather a plaster cast of it, as the bronze itself did not arrive until ten days later) in July 1922, it depicts a young soldier wearing a laurel victory wreath.

TRINITY STREET 1914

Looking south down the wonderful architectural hotch-potch of Trinity Street, with the medieval church of Great St Mary in the distance. Cambridge is renowned as a city of bicycles, and even in 1914 their presence was already conspicuous.

1ST EASTERN GENERAL HOSPITAL c1920

The 1st Eastern General Hospital was set up in Nevile's Court in Trinity College at the beginning of World War 1, with beds placed around the cloisters. As more and more injured men came back from the front, a larger hut hospital was built on the playing fields of King's and Clare Colleges, with 'open-air' wards such as this one housing the patients.

TRINITY STREET 1914 66891

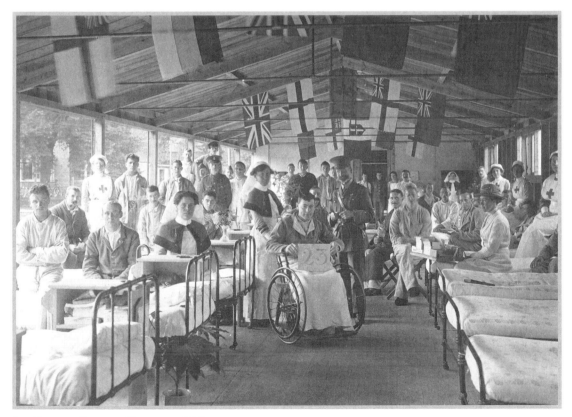

1ST EASTERN GENERAL HOSPITAL c1920 C14701

Christ's College

Corpus Christi College

manuel United Reformed Church   C. U. Press

TRUMPINGTON STREET c1955 C14064

Taken some fifty years after photograph No 61493, this view looks along Trumpington Street in the opposite direction, with Corpus Christi on the right hand side of the road, and King's in the distance.

PEMBROKE COLLEGE 1951 C14061

This view looks south down Trumpington Street, with the Front Court of Pembroke College on the left with its distinctive classically designed Wren Chapel. The Fitzwilliam Museum is in the distance on the right hand side of the road.

WESTMINSTER COLLEGE 1914 66896
Not part of the University, Westminster College is one of several theological colleges in Cambridge; this one is the college of the Presbyterian Church of England.

HOMERTON COLLEGE 1914 66900
When this photograph was taken, Homerton College was a teacher training college established some twenty years previously. In 1977 the college was recognised by the University, when a four-year degree course in Education was introduced.

King's Parade

KING'S PARADE 1911 63638

The ornate spires on the left form part of William Wilkins' screen which walls off the Front Court of King's College. In the background is the elegant classically designed Senate House, with Gonville and Caius College just beyond.

KING'S PARADE 1933 85547

Here, we are looking out onto King's Parade from the front of King's College. To the left is the Senate House, while the tower with four distinctive turrets belongs to the Church of Great St Mary. At the tailor's across the road, blazers are selling for 32/6 - £1.62 in today's money.

KING'S COLLEGE 1955 C14055

This view looks south along King's Parade, with King's College Chapel and the beautifully pinnacled screen and gatehouse leading to Front Court on the right. Although the architecture of the screen complements that of the chapel, the screen is in fact 300 years younger, built by the Gothic Revivalist William Wilkins.

SUSSEX STREET 1938 88523

Sussex Street, running between Sidney and Hobson Streets, was redeveloped in the 1930s, and finished off with these elegant colonnades. In recent years, the buildings at the far end of the street have been joined by a section which forms an archway.

HILLS ROAD, ROMAN CATHOLIC CHURCH 1931 84527a
The arrival of the railway in the mid 1840s led to considerable expansion in Cambridge, particularly on the southern and eastern sides. The Roman Catholic Church in Hills Road, built in 1890, was built to serve the rapidly expanding community in the town.

CHILDREN'S PADDLING POOL 1931
Newnham Paddling Pool in Lammas Land, pictured here with just a small handful of die-hard paddlers and bathers, and a park keeper looking on. Of course, the story would be different when a heatwave came along!

◆

HILLS ROAD 1931
In the distance, the tower of St Paul's church peers above the roof of the Globe Hotel. Nearby is the Perse School, established in 1625, and moved here from Free School Lane in 1890. Also nearby and out of view is the Scott Polar Research Institute, founded as a memorial to Captain Scott and his colleagues who died in their expedition to the South Pole.

CHILDREN'S PADDLING POOL 1931 84540

HILLS ROAD 1931 84528

KING'S PARADE 1921 70614
Gonville and Caius College is on the left,
along with James Gibbs' elegant Senate
House, where students are awarded their
degrees. Before the construction of the
Senate House in the early 18th century,
students received their degrees in the
Church of Great St Mary's, whose tower
dominates the right-hand side of the road.

CAIUS COLLEGE AND SENATE HOUSE 1890 26515

Hansom cabs line up on Senate House Hill, alongside the elegant classically styled Senate House, the 'Parliament' building for the University. Behind is Gonville and Caius (pronounced 'keys') College, the archway opening into Tree Court. In fact, Dr John Caius, who refounded the College in 1557, was a Norwich man whose family name was originally Keys; later, it was Latinized, as was the fashion of the day.

KING'S PARADE 1890 26496
The elegant classically-designed
Senate House is on the right, with
King's College Chapel to the left.
The Senate House, designed by
James Gibbs, is the meeting place
of the governing body of the
University, and is also the place
where degrees are conferred.

CORPUS CHRISTI COLLEGE c1955 C14058
This view looks north along Trumpington Street. Corpus Christi College is on the right hand side, with St Botolph's church just in the foreground. In the distance are the unmistakable slender spires of King's College Chapel.

VIEW OF YARD 1914 66894
With houses crowded together, yards like this were not uncommon in Cambridge. There may not be anything in the way of a garden, but the flower boxes and tubs certainly help to brighten up what otherwise appears to be a parking place for bicycles and hand carts.

LEYS SCHOOL 1890 26592
The Leys was founded by Methodists as a boys' school
run on Christian principles. It counts the former BBC
foreign correspondent turned independent MP Martin
Bell as one of its scholars in more recent times.

EIGHTS 1909 61510

Cambridge has a long history of rowing. Because the River Cam itself is not wide enough for conventional races, races called 'Bumps' are held. Eights such as this one start about one and a half lengths behind one another, and each boat has to catch up with the one in front, thus 'bumping' it.

THE CAM 1914 66903a
These days, gravel prevents the less experienced punter from having his pole stick in the mud. When the colleges enclosed the Backs, the towpaths became obstructed; gravel was spread on the bed of the River Cam so that horses towing barges could wade up the river instead.

The River Cam

MATHEMATICAL BRIDGE c1955

The curious Mathematical Bridge across the Cam, built on geometric principles, and originally held together - so the story goes - without any fixing devices. Apparently when it was taken apart at the turn of the century to discover the principles upon which it was built, those who dismantled it could not reassemble it without the use of bolts.

❖

JESUS LOCK 1925

Jesus Lock is the limit of navigation on the River Cam for powered craft. The river above here is that which flows past the colleges, travelled on there at a much more leisurely rate by rowing boats and punts. The footbridge was built in 1892.

MATHEMATICAL BRIDGE c1955 C14080

JESUS LOCK 1925 78731b

THE CAM, TRINITY BRIDGE 1914 66902a

It just goes to show it is not only the roads which suffer from traffic jams. Boating and punting on the Cam has long been a popular pastime, and it is no different now from when this photograph was taken.

GREEN DRAGON FERRY 1909 61517

There is a real art to punting. If you do it properly, both forward motion and steering is provided by the pole. But as these boaters opposite the Green Dragon pub in Water Street in Chesterton demonstrate, it does take some practice, which is why a paddle can come in handy for the less experienced. There were two ferries operating across the river here to Stourbridge Common, the larger of the two able to take a horse and cart. Both ferries ceased operating in 1935 when a footbridge was built here.

THE BACKS 1890 26495

The Backs of Cambridge are probably as well known as the colleges themselves. Immaculately kept lawns sweep down to the peaceful River Cam. The scene is dominated by the breathtaking Perpendicular splendour of King's College Chapel.

HORNINGSEA, LOCK GATES ON THE RIVER CAM c1955 H443012

North-east of Cambridge, the River Cam quickly becomes wooded on either side, setting an attractive scene here at Baits Bite Lock. The weir on the left marks the difference in height between the two levels of the river. The lock gates to the right allow the passage of boats between the two.

MADINGLEY, THE CHURCH 1909 61525

The church of St Mary Magdalene is mainly 13th and 14th-century, with beautiful stained glass windows dating from the 16th century. The nearby Elizabethan Madingley Hall was the residence for both Edward VII and George VI during their time in Cambridge as undergraduates.

MARSHALL AIRPORT 1938 88520

Cambridge's Marshall Airport was built just the year before this photograph was taken. The Marshall family first set up in Cambridge in 1909 with an engineering company to provide car maintenance and coach building work to the rich undergraduates of the University.

GRANTCHESTER, THE CHURCH 1929 81771a

The last two lines of Rupert Brooke's poem 'The Old Vicarage, Grantchester' have immortalised the church: 'Stands the church clock at ten to three, And is there honey still for tea?' It is believed that the clock was actually broken when the poet was living in Grantchester. For years after Brooke's death, the clock was kept at that time as a memorial to him.

GRANTCHESTER
The Old Mill 1914
'And laughs the immortal river still Under the mill, under the mill'. So wrote the poet Rupert Brooke about Grantchester's mill. The river may well be immortal, but the mill certainly was not. It burned down in 1928.

◆

GRANTCHESTER
The Village 1914
Intentional or unnoticed? The photographer has managed to capture someone either entering or leaving his or her house. A few seconds either way, and the photograph would have had a person in it to add a touch more interest!

GRANTCHESTER, THE OLD MILL 1914 66908a

GRANTCHESTER, THE VILLAGE 1914 66908

GRANTCHESTER, THE VILLAGE 1929 81768
The poet Rupert Brooke died in the Dardanelles in 1915. In the years that followed, the village became a
popular place to visit, with a number of places of refreshment springing up.

MADINGLEY, THE HALL c1950 M5002
This beautiful Tudor mansion was built at the end of the reign of Henry VIII by the successful lawyer Sir John
Hynde, partly from materials salvaged when they pulled down the church of St Etheldreda in Histon. In 1756,
the owners of the hall commissioned Capability Brown to lay out a park.

MADINGLEY, THE VILLAGE 1909 61523
Thatched roofs predominate in this turn-of-the-century view of Madingley. The footpaths beside the road have not yet developed into raised paths with kerb stones, but are at least demarcated by a line of grass.

MADINGLEY, THE CHURCH c1955 M5006
Madingley is a typical example of an estate village which was remodelled in order to improve the view from the landlord's mansion. When the Cotton family commissioned Capability Brown to design a park in 1756, he cut a swathe through the village, separating the church and a couple of farms and cottages from the rest of the village.

MADINGLEY, THE RUINED WINDMILL 1909 61524
Looking very much a shadow of its former self, this windmill would have ground corn. In common with other mills in the area, it is a post mill, with the mill revolving round the central post.

FULBOURN, HIGH STREET c1950 F104008
One hopes that the Express parcel service
fared better than the shop's window
advertising, which suffers from a number
of missing letters! Down by the crossroads
is the Six Bells public house, while to
the left, the church is one of only two in
England dedicated to Saint Vigor.

FULBOURN, HIGH STREET c1950 F104002
Peering just around the corner of the house on the right is a petrol pump. This was quite acceptable in the 1950s perhaps, but is not legal now.

FULBOURN, THE MANOR c1955 F104025
A neatly manicured gravel driveway in front of the manor house in Fulbourn. It has been lived in by the Townley family since the 18th century, although the house itself dates back to around a century earlier.

TRUMPINGTON, THE VILLAGE 1914 66910
Thatched cottages abound in this view; at this time, Trumpington was a village separate from Cambridge.
Although only visible from its sign in this picture, the Green Man is a magnificent timbered public house.

FEN DITTON, THE VILLAGE 1914 66916
A set of stone steps leading nowhere might seem a rather odd thing to have on the roadside. They were, of course,
designed to make life easier when using transport of the four-legged variety; although by the time this photograph
was taken, the motor car was beginning to make its presence felt. Home Farm can be seen in the foreground.

HISTON, THE CHURCH 1965 H442002

There used to be two churches in Histon, but St Etheldreda's, not far from this one, St Andrew's, was demolished in 1588 to provide materials for a new wing at Madingley Hall.

HISTON, HIGH STREET c1965 H442003

Filling stations are no longer allowed to have their pumps directly adjacent to pavements, but in the days of the dependable ash-framed Morris Traveller, it was pretty much the norm. Histon is where Mr Chivers started making jam in a barn in 1873.

IMPINGTON, THE CHURCH c1965 H442011
As with so many churches, St Andrew's in Impington exhibits an interesting blend of styles. The chancel was extensively rebuilt in the latter part of the 19th century, but the rest is considerably older, including the timber-framed porch, which dates back to late medieval times.

TEVERSHAM, ALL SAINTS' CHURCH c1965 T298001
Here we experience the tranquillity of the churchyard in Teversham, just a stone's throw from the bustle of nearby Cambridge. The church's Jacobean pulpit came from the neighbouring parish church in Cherry Hinton.

TEVERSHAM
High Street c1965
Post-war expansion of Cambridge pushed the suburbs into outlying villages. We can see early signs of the requirement to control traffic flow: the now ubiquitous Keep Left bollards.

◆

GREAT SHELFORD
The Village 1914
There are some obvious posers in this photograph. Peering over the thatched roof is the battlemented octagon of the village church, rebuilt after two collapses in the 18th century.

TEVERSHAM, HIGH STREET c1965 T298004

GREAT SHELFORD, THE VILLAGE 1914 66913

GREAT SHELFORD, THE VILLAGE 1914 66914a
With their knee-length breeches and caps, the word that comes to mind is 'urchins'. More to the point, one wonders just what it was they were conspiring about when the photographer set up to take this photograph!

GREAT SHELFORD, WOOLLARDS LANE c1955 G278012
The cyclists here obviously felt sufficiently safe not
to worry too much about hugging the kerb and
avoiding brushes with the traffic. The practice of
parking a bicycle by leaning it on one pedal against
the kerb is rarely seen these days.

Index

The Francis Frith Collection Titles

www.francisfrith.co.uk

The Francis Frith Collection publishes over 100 new titles each year. A selection of those currently available is listed below. For latest catalogue please contact The Francis Frith Collection **Town Books** 96 pages, approximately 75 photos. **County and Themed Books** 128 pages, approximately 135 photos (unless specified). All titles hardback with laminated case and jacket, except those indicated pb (paperback)

Accrington Old and New
Alderley Edge and Wilmslow
Amersham, Chesham and Rickmansworth
Andover
Around Abergavenny
Around Alton
Aylesbury
Barnstaple
Bedford
Bedfordshire
Berkshire Living Memories
Berkshire PA
Blackpool Pocket Album
Bognor Regis
Bournemouth
Bradford
Bridgend
Bridport
Brighton and Hove
Bristol
Buckinghamshire
Calne Living Memories
Camberley PA
Canterbury Cathedral
Cardiff Old and New
Chatham and the Medway Towns
Chelmsford
Chepstow Then and Now
Cheshire
Cheshire Living Memories
Chester
Chesterfield
Chigwell
Christchurch
Churches of East Cornwall
Clevedon
Clitheroe
Corby Living Memories
Cornish Coast
Cornwall Living Memories
Cotswold Living Memories
Cotswold Pocket Album
Coulsdon, Chipstead and Woodmanstern
County Durham
Cromer, Sheringham and Holt
Dartmoor Pocket Album
Derby
Derbyshire
Derbyshire Living Memories
Devon
Devon Churches
Dorchester

Dorset Coast PA
Dorset Living Memories
Dorset Villages
Down the Dart
Down the Severn
Down the Thames
Dunmow, Thaxted and Finchingfield
Durham
East Anglia PA
East Devon
East Grinstead
Edinburgh
Ely and The Fens
Essex PA
Essex Second Selection
Essex: The London Boroughs
Exeter
Exmoor
Falmouth
Farnborough, Fleet and Aldershot
Folkestone
Frome
Furness and Cartmel Peninsulas
Glamorgan
Glasgow
Glastonbury
Gloucester
Gloucestershire
Greater Manchester
Guildford
Hailsham
Hampshire
Harrogate
Hastings and Bexhill
Haywards Heath Living Memories
Heads of the Valleys
Heart of Lancashire PA
Helston
Herefordshire
Horsham
Humberside PA
Huntingdon, St Neots and St Ives
Hythe, Romney Marsh and Ashford
Ilfracombe
Ipswich PA
Isle of Wight
Isle of Wight Living Memories
King's Lynn
Kingston upon Thames
Lake District PA
Lancashire Living Memories
Lancashire Villages

Available from your local bookshop or from the publisher

The Francis Frith Collection Titles (continued)

Lancaster, Morecombe and Heysham Pocket Album
Leeds PA
Leicester
Leicestershire
Lincolnshire Living Memoires
Lincolnshire Pocket Album
Liverpool and Merseyside
London PA
Ludlow
Maidenhead
Maidstone
Malmesbury
Manchester PA
Marlborough
Matlock
Merseyside Living Memories
Nantwich and Crewe
New Forest
Newbury Living Memories
Newquay to St Ives
North Devon Living Memories
North London
North Wales
North Yorkshire
Northamptonshire
Northumberland
Northwich
Nottingham
Nottinghamshire PA
Oakham
Odiham Then and Now
Oxford Pocket Album
Oxfordshire
Padstow
Pembrokeshire
Penzance
Petersfield Then and Now
Plymouth
Poole and Sandbanks
Preston PA
Ramsgate Old and New
Reading Pocket Album
Redditch Living Memories
Redhill to Reigate
Rhondda Valley Living Mems
Richmond
Ringwood
Rochdale
Romford PA
Salisbury PA
Scotland
Scottish Castles
Sevenoaks and Tonbridge
Sheffield and South Yorkshire PA
Shropshire
Somerset
South Devon Coast
South Devon Living Memories
South East London
Southampton PA
Southend PA

Southport
Southwold to Aldeburgh
Stourbridge Living Memories
Stratford upon Avon
Stroud
Suffolk
Suffolk PA
Surrey Living Memories
Sussex
Sutton
Swanage and Purbeck
Swansea Pocket Album
Swindon Living Memories
Taunton
Teignmouth
Tenby and Saundersfoot
Tiverton
Torbay
Truro
Uppingham
Villages of Kent
Villages of Surrey
Villages of Sussex PA
Wakefield and the Five Towns Living Memories
Warrington
Warwick
Warwickshire PA
Wellingborough Living Memories
Wells
Welsh Castles
West Midlands PA
West Wiltshire Towns
West Yorkshire
Weston-super-Mare
Weymouth
Widnes and Runcorn
Wiltshire Churches
Wiltshire Living memories
Wiltshire PA
Wimborne
Winchester PA
Windermere
Windsor
Wirral
Wokingham and Bracknell
Woodbridge
Worcester
Worcestershire
Worcestershire Living Memories
Wyre Forest
York PA
Yorkshire
Yorkshire Coastal Memories
Yorkshire Dales
Yorkshire Revisited

See Frith books on the internet at www.francisfrith.co.uk

FRITH PRODUCTS & SERVICES

Francis Frith would doubtless be pleased to know that the pioneering publishing venture he started in 1860 still continues today. Over a hundred and forty years later, The Francis Frith Collection continues in the same innovative tradition and is now one of the foremost publishers of vintage photographs in the world. Some of the current activities include:

Interior Decoration

Today Frith's photographs can be seen framed and as giant wall murals in thousands of pubs, restaurants, hotels, banks, retail stores and other public buildings throughout the country. In every case they enhance the unique local atmosphere of the places they depict and provide reminders of gentler days in an increasingly busy and frenetic world.

Product Promotions

Frith products are used by many major companies to promote the sales of their own products or to reinforce their own history and heritage. Frith promotions have been used by Hovis bread, Courage beers, Scots Porage Oats, Colman's mustard, Cadbury's foods, Mellow Birds coffee, Dunhill pipe tobacco, Guinness, and Bulmer's Cider.

Genealogy and Family History

As the interest in family history and roots grows world-wide, more and more people are turning to Frith's photographs of Great Britain for images of the towns, villages and streets where their ancestors lived; and, of course, photographs of the churches and chapels where their ancestors were christened, married and buried are an essential part of every genealogy tree and family album.

Frith Products

All Frith photographs are available Framed or just as Mounted Prints and Posters (size 23 x 16 inches). These may be ordered from the address below. From time to time other products - Address Books, Calendars, Table Mats, etc - are available.

The Internet

Already ninety thousand Frith photographs can be viewed and purchased on the internet through the Frith websites and a myriad of partner sites.

For more detailed information on Frith companies and products, look at these sites:

www.francisfrith.co.uk
www.francisfrith.com
(for North American visitors)

See the complete list of Frith Books at:

www.francisfrith.co.uk

This web site is regularly updated with the latest list of publications from The Francis Frith Collection. If you wish to buy books relating to another part of the country that your local bookshop does not stock, you may purchase on-line.

For further information, trade, or author enquiries please contact us at the address below:
The Francis Frith Collection, Frith's Barn, Teffont, Salisbury, Wiltshire, England SP3 5QP.
Tel: +44 (0)1722 716 376 Fax: +44 (0)1722 716 881 Email: sales@francisfrith.co.uk

See Frith books on the internet at www.francisfrith.co.uk